OCT   2015

★ HOCKEY SUPERSTARS ★

SIDNEY CROSBY

BY MICHAEL BURGAN

CAPSTONE PRESS
a capstone imprint

Sports Illustrated Kids Hockey Superstars are published by Capstone Press,
1710 Roe Crest Drive, North Mankato, Minnesota 56003.
www.capstonepub.com

Library of Congress Cataloging-in-Publication Data
Burgan, Michael.
Sidney Crosby / by Michael Burgan.
    pages cm. – (Sports illustrated kids. Hockey superstars)
Includes bibliographical references and index.
Summary: "Details the life and career of hockey superstar Sidney Crosby"—
Provided by publisher.
ISBN 978-1-4914-2138-3 (library binding)
1. Crosby, Sidney, 1987—Juvenile literature. 2. Hockey players—Canada—
Biography—Juvenile literature. I. Title.
GV848.5.C76.B86 2015
796.962092—dc23
[B]   2014032830

Editorial Credits
Brenda Haugen, editor; Ted Williams, designer; Eric Gohl, media researcher;
Morgan Walters, production specialist

Photo Credits
AP Photo: The Canadian Press/Mike Dembeck, 10; Dreamstime: Jerry Coli, 1;
Newscom: Icon SMI/Darren Carroll, 15, Reuters/Chris Wattie, 17, ZUMA Press/
Marlin Levison, 13; Sports Illustrated: Damian Strohmeyer, 4–5, 6–7, 9, David E.
Klutho, cover, back cover, 18, 19, 21, 23, 24, 26, 30–31 (background), Simon Bruty,
28–29, 32 (background)

Design Elements
Shutterstock

Source Note
Page 11, line 11: Gare Joyce. *Sidney Crosby: Taking the Game by Storm*. Markhan,
Ontario, Canada: Fitzhenry & Whiteside, 2005, p. 38.

Printed in the United States of America in Stevens Point, Wisconsin.
092014   008479WZS15

TABLE OF CONTENTS

CHAPTER 1

THE GOLDEN GOAL

Sidney Crosby was living his dream. The Pittsburgh Penguins **center** was playing hockey in the 2010 Winter Olympics with a chance to help Canada win a gold medal. Even better, the Games were being held in Vancouver, Canada. Canadian fans filled the hockey arena to root for Crosby and his teammates.

center—the player who participates in a face-off at the beginning of play

Crosby's Olympic adventure began February 16. Canada easily defeated Norway 8-0. Crosby netted three assists in the game. He won Canada's next game against Switzerland with a **shoot-out** goal that broke a 2-2 tie. But Canada lost the following game to the United States, which forced Canada to play in the qualification round in the playoffs.

shoot-out—a method of breaking a tie score at the end of overtime play

Canada pounded Germany 8-2 in the qualification round. The momentum carried over into the next round, where Canada beat Russia 7-3. After beating Slovakia 3-2 in the semifinals, Canada was set for a rematch with the United States in the gold medal game.

Canada scored a goal in each of the first two periods. With just 30 seconds left in the game, the Canadians clung to a 2-1 lead. Then American Zach Parise scored a goal, and the game went to overtime. The team that scored first would win the gold medal. If no one scored, Crosby would likely be taking part in another shoot-out. But Crosby made sure the game would end before then.

Nearly eight minutes into overtime, Crosby skated toward the U.S. goal. Four Americans dashed toward him. Crosby rushed forward and pushed the puck toward the net. Goaltender Ryan Miller easily knocked it aside.

Crosby chased down the puck and passed it to Jarome Iginla. Then Crosby dashed toward the net shouting, "Iggy!"—Iginla's nickname. Iginla fell to the ice but managed to pass the puck back to Crosby. In one smooth motion, Crosby flicked the puck between Miller's legs. The Canadians won the gold medal!

Sportswriters called Crosby's shot "the Golden Goal." Some thought it was the greatest moment in sports for 2010. Crosby said scoring the goal felt like a dream.

Crosby would play for Canada again in the 2014 Olympics. He also would lead the National Hockey League (NHL) in scoring several times and emerge as one of its top stars. But few moments in hockey have ever matched his Golden Goal. It was another highlight of Crosby's young but great career.

FAST FACT

Crosby scored four goals and added three assists during the 2010 Olympics. His seven points tied for the second-highest total on the Canadian team.

points—a player's total number of goals and assists

Sidney's family, Trina, Taylor, and Troy, posed in front of a sign welcoming visitors to their hometown in 2008.

CHAPTER 2

AN EARLY START

Many Canadian kids learn how to skate at an early age. Sidney Crosby was no different. He was born in Cole Harbour, Nova Scotia, August 7, 1987. Just a little more than three years later, he was wearing his first skates. At 5 years old, he was playing hockey against older kids. For many years he would be the youngest player on the ice every time he played.

As a young player, Sidney often practiced his shooting skills. Sometimes his grandmother would sit in a living room chair and play goalie as Sidney tried to shoot the puck past her. He said years later, "She was tough to beat." Sidney also took countless shots at a net set up in the basement.

FAST FACT

Sidney's father, Troy, was a goalie. Troy was drafted by the NHL's Montreal Canadiens in 1984. The Canadiens were Sidney's favorite team when he was growing up.

draft—to choose a person to join a sports organization or team

Sidney played hockey as much as he could, and he kept getting better. He controlled the puck well and made **accurate** passes. Sidney also showed excellent sportsmanship. He didn't brag about his skills or look down on other kids who weren't as good.

accurate—able to hit the spot being aimed for

FAST FACT

Crosby's younger sister, Taylor, also plays hockey. She is a goalie and would like to play in the Olympics for Canada some day. At home in Cole Harbour, she and her famous brother sometimes play hockey together.

A FAMOUS CLOTHES DRYER

An old clothes dryer sits in the Nova Scotia Sport Hall of Fame. It once sat in the Crosby family's basement. The dryer was next to the goal that Sidney used for practice. When Sidney missed the net, the puck hit the dryer. Over the years the dryer became covered with dents and black marks.

Goalie Taylor Crosby practiced with her high school team.

Later some people believed that Sidney tried to shoot into the dryer. On a U.S. television show, Crosby was asked to shoot pucks into a different dryer. But Crosby said his aim back in Cole Harbour was not to put the puck inside the dryer. He wanted to hit the net. Crosby's mother was OK with the dryer getting hit—as long as it still worked.

Sidney started playing for the Dartmouth Subways in Nova Scotia when he was 14 years old. Dartmouth and other teams in its league had mostly 16- and 17-year-olds. Despite playing against older players, Sidney scored 95 goals in 74 games and recorded 98 assists.

During the 2002–03 season, Sidney went to Shattuck-St. Mary's, a high school in Minnesota. He led Shattuck's hockey team with 162 points and helped it win a national championship.

Sidney was drafted by the Rimouski Oceanic in 2003. The team was part of the Canadian Hockey League (CHL). So Sidney came back to Canada to finish high school and play hockey. It proved to be a good decision. In two seasons with Rimouski, Sidney racked up 303 points and twice was named Player of the Year.

Sidney also began playing international hockey. He skated for Canada in the International Ice Hockey World Junior Championship. The tournament features players under 20 years old. Sidney was 17 when he helped Canada win the gold medal in 2005. He scored six goals and had three assists in six games.

Soon Sidney would have the chance to show his skills against the world's best pro players. He was ready to join the NHL.

Crosby played for Rimouski for two years.

FAST FACT

Rimouski is in Quebec, a part of Canada where most people speak French. Crosby learned French while he was there. He has given interviews in both French and English.

CHAPTER 3

THE KID TAKES CHARGE

NHL teams were preparing for the draft in July 2005. Sidney Crosby was clearly the best player available. In a **lottery** the Pittsburgh Penguins won the right to take him.

The Penguins were owned by Mario Lemieux. He was still playing at 40 years old even though he had battled injuries and illness during his career. Now he was eager to play alongside Crosby.

Crosby turned 18 soon after the draft. He was often called "Sid the Kid." People in the NHL hoped he would bring new interest to the game, and reporters constantly asked him questions. The Penguins counted on him to bring fans to their arena.

lottery—a way of randomly choosing which team will pick first in the draft

FAST FACT

When he came to Pittsburgh, Crosby moved in with Mario Lemieux and his family. Sometimes Lemieux's wife, Nathalie, cooked Crosby special meals before games. Crosby lived with the Lemieuxs during several seasons.

Another **rookie** was also expected to do well that season. Russian **winger** Alexander Ovechkin was the league's top draft pick in 2004, but he hadn't played yet because a **lockout** had shut down the league. Through the 2005–06 season, Ovechkin and Crosby would compete to be the league's top rookie.

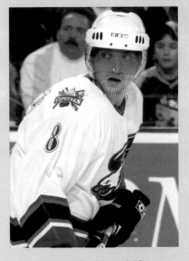

Alexander Ovechkin

Crosby's pro career got off to a good start. He tallied an assist in his first game. He continued to improve during the season and ended with 102 points. He was the youngest player ever to score 100 points or more in a season. Despite Crosby's efforts, the Penguins still struggled and failed to reach the playoffs. Crosby also missed out on being named Rookie of the Year. The award went to Ovechkin, who scored 106 points that season.

rookie—a first-year player

winger—a type of forward who usually stays near the sides of the zone

lockout—a period of time in which owners prevent players from reporting to their teams; owners do not pay players during lockouts and no games are played

FAST FACT

Crosby and Ovechkin first played against each other in the 2005 World Junior Championship.

The next season Crosby led the NHL with 120 points, despite playing the last six weeks with a broken bone in his foot. He won the Hart Trophy, which goes to the league's best player. The Penguins recognized Crosby's hard work and leadership. Before the 2007–08 season, they named him team captain. At just 19 years old, Crosby became the youngest captain in the NHL history.

During his first season as captain, Crosby missed almost 30 games due to an ankle injury. But he was healthy for the playoffs. Crosby led the Penguins to the **Stanley Cup** Final where they faced the Detroit Red Wings. Though Pittsburgh lost the series four games to two, Crosby led all players in the playoffs in assists with 21 and points with 27.

Crosby scored 103 points in the 2008–09 season, again leading his team to the playoffs. After defeating the Philadelphia Flyers in the first round, the Penguins faced the Capitals. A 5-4 Washington victory in Game 6 pushed the tough series to a deciding Game 7. Crosby was in fine form, scoring two goals and helping the Penguins win the series.

After beating the Carolina Hurricanes, the Penguins again faced the Red Wings for the Stanley Cup. In a deciding Game 7, the Penguins pulled off a dramatic 2-1 win. Crosby had just one goal in the series, but during the playoffs he led all scorers with 15 goals.

The Penguins had won the Stanley Cup for the first time since 1992. Crosby held the Cup up high. He was the youngest captain in NHL history to lead his team to the ultimate prize.

Stanley Cup—the trophy given each year to the NHL champion

21

CROSBY ★ CROSBY ★ CROSBY ★ CROSBY ★ CROSBY ★ CROSBY ★ CROSBY ★ CROSBY ★ CROS

HELPING OTHERS BACK HOME

Crosby started the Sidney Crosby Foundation in 2009 to help kids in Nova Scotia. One of the projects the foundation paid for was a lounge for teenagers at a Halifax children's hospital. Money from the foundation helped fix up the lounge and make it bigger.

During the 2009–10 season, Crosby really showed his scoring talents. He netted 51 goals—the first time he reached the 50-goal level in the NHL. But the Penguins did not repeat as Stanley Cup champions. They were one of the top teams during the regular season and won their first playoff series against the Ottawa Senators. But in the second round, Pittsburgh lost to the Montreal Canadiens in seven games. Crosby had a total of 19 points in the two series.

It was a disappointment for Crosby after leading his team to a championship the previous year. But the next year Crosby would face an even bigger challenge.

donate—to give something as a gift

Crosby and his foundation have raised money in several ways. In 2012 Crosby played a charity hockey game in Cole Harbour with his childhood friends. Crosby has also **donated** his own money. Each player on Canada's 2010 ice hockey team had received $20,000 for winning the gold medal. Crosby gave his money to his foundation.

CHAPTER 4

FIGHTING BACK

Crosby scored at an amazing pace for two months early in the 2010–11 season. He netted two goals in a 3-2 win against the Anaheim Ducks on November 5. He went on to notch at least one point in the next 24 games. It was a scoring streak the league had not seen for almost 20 years. During those 25 games, Crosby scored 26 goals and recorded 24 assists.

The rest of the season saw Crosby battling injuries. He suffered two head injuries in January and missed the remainder of the season. He also missed the start of the next season, finally playing a few games in November. But dizzy spells forced him to sit again. Some people wondered if he would ever play pro hockey again.

A SERIOUS CONCERN IN SPORTS

On January 5, 2011, an opposing player sent Crosby crashing into the boards headfirst. The check and a previous injury left Crosby with a serious brain injury called a concussion. A concussion can make a person feel dizzy, cause headaches, or make it hard to see. Crosby endured the effects of his injury for months.

check—a legal hit with the body to try to force a player away from the puck

Finally, in March 2012, Crosby returned to the ice. But disaster struck again the next year. During a March 2013 game, the puck bounced off a stick and slammed into Crosby's face.

The puck knocked out several teeth and bloodied Crosby's face. Later he learned the shot also broke his jaw. Crosby did not play for more than a month. The season had already been shortened. It had started three months late because of another lockout between the players and owners.

The Penguins finished the short season with a good record and made the playoffs. Crosby returned to the ice for Game 2 of the Penguins' series against the New York Islanders. He quickly proved he was back to form, scoring two goals in the game's first period. The Penguins went on to win the series four games to two.

They made even quicker work of the Ottawa Senators in the next round, defeating them four games to one. But the Penguins lost in four games to the Boston Bruins in the conference final. In 14 playoff games, Crosby scored seven goals and added eight assists.

FAST FACT

Crosby signed a new contract with the Penguins in 2012 that would give him $104 million over the next 12 years.

Crosby was finally healthy again when the 2013–14 season began. He was named captain of Canada's hockey team for the 2014 Olympics. Though Crosby scored just one goal during the Games, Canada once again took home the gold medal.

Crosby had another great season in the NHL. He again scored more than 100 points and led the league. Although Pittsburgh only reached the second round of the playoffs, Crosby won his second Hart Trophy as the NHL's **Most Valuable Player** (MVP). Crosby was no longer "Sid the Kid." He was a grown man ready to play great hockey for many more years to come.

most valuable player—an honor given to the best player each season

GLOSSARY

accurate (AK-yuh-ruht)—able to hit the spot being aimed for

center (SEN-tur)—the player who participates in a face-off at the beginning of play

check (CHEK)—a legal hit with the body to try to force a player away from the puck

donate (DOH-nayt)—to give something as a gift

draft (DRAFT)—to choose a person to join a sports organization or team

lockout (LOK-out)—a period of time in which owners prevent players from reporting to their teams; owners do not pay players during lockouts and no games are played

lottery (LOT-ur-ee)—a way of randomly choosing which team will pick first in the draft

most valuable player (MOHST VAL-yoo-buhl PLAY-ur)—an honor given to the best player each season

points (POYNTZ)—a player's total number of goals and assists

rookie (RUK-ee)—a first-year player

shoot-out (SHOOT-owt)—a method of breaking a tie score at the end of overtime play

Stanley Cup (STAN-lee KUP)—the trophy given each year to the NHL champion

winger (WING-ur)—a type of forward who usually stays near the sides of the zone

READ MORE

Burns, Kylie. *Sidney Crosby.* Superstars! New York: Crabtree Publishing Company, 2014.

Frederick, Shane. *Hockey Legends in the Making.* Sports Illustrated Kids: Legends in the Making. North Mankato, Minn.: Capstone Press, 2014.

Gitlin, Marty. *The Stanley Cup: All About Pro Hockey's Biggest Event.* Sports Illustrated Kids: Winner Takes All. North Mankato, Minn.: Capstone Press, 2013.

Labrecque, Ellen. *Pittsburgh Penguins.* Mankato, Minn.: Child's World, 2011.

INTERNET SITES

FactHound offers a safe, fun way to find Internet sites related to this book. All of the sites on FactHound have been researched by our staff.

Here's all you do:

Visit *www.facthound.com*

Type in this code: 9781491421383

Super-cool stuff! Check out projects, games and lots more at **www.capstonekids.com**

INDEX